# HOW TO SURVIVE THE ZOMBIE APOCALYPSE

BEN JACKSON

This book is not a guarantee of survival if there is a zombie apocalypse. The author does not condone or recommend violence or the use of weaponry as practice for zombie fights. We are not responsible for any accidents, damage to persons or property and/or loss of life occurring from the text below.

All attempts have been made to verify the information contained in this book, but the author and publisher do not bear any responsibility for errors or omissions. Any perceived negative connotation of any individual, group, or company is purely unintentional. Furthermore, this book is intended as entertainment only and, as such, any and all responsibility for actions taken upon reading this book lies with the reader alone and not with the author or publisher. This book is not intended as medical, legal, or business advice and the reader alone holds sole responsibility for any consequences of any actions taken after reading this book. Additionally, it is the reader's responsibility alone and not the author's or publisher's to ensure that all applicable laws and regulations for business practice are adhered to. Lastly, I sometimes utilize affiliate links in the content of this book and therefore, if you make a purchase through these links, I will gain a small commission.

Copyright © 2015 by Ben Jackson

Indie Publishing Group

All rights reserved. No part of this publication may be reproduced, distributed, or transmitted in any form or by any means, including photocopying, recording, or other electronic or mechanical methods, without the prior written permission of the publisher, except in the case of brief quotations embodied in critical reviews and certain other noncommercial uses permitted by copyright law.

*To my amazing wife, who is my best friend and soul mate.*

*She has always believed in me and pushed me to be better in everything that I do.*

# Contents

**INTRODUCTION** . . . . . . . . . . . . . . . . . . . . . . . . . . . . . . . . . . . . . . . . 1

**CHAPTER ONE** . . . . . . . . . . . . . . . . . . . . . . . . . . . . . . . . . . . . . . . . . 3
    Different Types of Zombies - The Four Main Four Types

**CHAPTER TWO** . . . . . . . . . . . . . . . . . . . . . . . . . . . . . . . . . . . . . . . 13
    Part 1. Staying Put
    Part 2. Keeping Mobile

**CHAPTER THREE** . . . . . . . . . . . . . . . . . . . . . . . . . . . . . . . . . . . . . 25
    Preparation & Supplies

**CHAPTER FOUR** . . . . . . . . . . . . . . . . . . . . . . . . . . . . . . . . . . . . . . 39
    Preferred Zombie & Defense Weapons

**CHAPTER FIVE** . . . . . . . . . . . . . . . . . . . . . . . . . . . . . . . . . . . . . . . 47
    Do It Solo Or In A Group

**CHAPTER SIX** . . . . . . . . . . . . . . . . . . . . . . . . . . . . . . . . . . . . . . . . 51
    How To Form A Survival Group

**CHAPTER SEVEN** . . . . . . . . . . . . . . . . . . . . . . . . . . . . . . . . . . . . . 57
    Best Vehicles for Post-Apocalyptic Travel

**CHAPTER EIGHT** . . . . . . . . . . . . . . . . . . . . . . . . . . . . . . . . . . . . . 61
    Zombie Misconceptions

**CHAPTER NINE** . . . . . . . . . . . . . . . . . . . . . . . . . . . . . . . . . . . . . . 67
    Zombie Survival Tips to Keep You Alive

**CHAPTER TEN** . . . . . . . . . . . . . . . . . . . . . . . . . . . . . . . . . . . . . . . 71
    Zombies That You're Likely to Encounter

**CONCLUSION** . . . . . . . . . . . . . . . . . . . . . . . . . . . . . . . . . . . . . . . 75

**REFERENCES** . . . . . . . . . . . . . . . . . . . . . . . . . . . . . . . . . . . . . . . . 79

# Introduction

So the worst has happened zombies are walking the earth looking for fresh victims. Hopefully you downloaded this book beforehand and have studied it carefully, otherwise it could already be too late. This isn't the bible of dealing with zombies, but I've tried to get as close to one as I can get. Obviously some of the information in this book is tongue in cheek; the rest, well…it could just save your life one day.

More and more we see the threat of a zombie apocalypse becoming a reality. Movies, television shows, plays and even on the news. We live in a world where chemical accidents or a science experiment gone wrong is a very real possibility. Everyone assumes that they know exactly what they're doing, but when you think about it, some of the most important scientific discoveries of all time were made by accident.

Penicillin was discovered in 1928 by Alexander Fleming returning to his lab after a holiday and discovering a strange fungus on a sample he had accidentally left out. The man who invented Coca-Cola wasn't an amazing businessman or someone out to find the most popular fizzy drink of all time. John Pemberton was just a guy looking to cure the common headache. When his lab assistant accidentally mixed coca leaves with cola nuts and carbonated water, Coca-Cola was born. He died just two years later, but Coca-Cola is arguably the most well-known drink in the world today. So, is it that unlikely that a man in a laboratory somewhere, splicing DNA together to cure cancer, could accidentally unleash a plague of walking dead? Nope, it isn't that much of a stretch at all.

Luckily, as I write this there hasn't been a swarm of zombies that have overrun the earth. However, if it isn't zombies, then it will most likely be a virus or infectious disease of some sort or another. There are a lot of different schools of thought when it comes to zombies - what they eat, how they function, how quick or slow they move and how to kill them. Everyone is an expert, yet at the same time no one is. That old saying, "Always be prepared" has this one pretty damn right. Another saying I like is, "Assumption is the mother of all f#*k ups." So be prepared for everything, and assume nothing when it comes to those unholy, flesh-eating creatures of the night.

## Chapter One

# DIFFERENT TYPES OF ZOMBIES – THE FOUR MAIN TYPES

There are four main types of zombies that you could not only encounter, but have to kill. They are Haitian & Voodoo zombies, Chemical zombies, Parasitic zombies and Viral zombies. I'm going to give you a detailed description of where each of these come from, what things you need to be aware of, and teach you how to recognize the symptoms before they turn into a zombie. We'll go into more specific details on how to kill them and with what weapons later on in the book.

## *Part 1. Haitian or Voodoo Zombies*

In Haiti, zombies have more religious connotations rather than the traditional plague of the dead sweeping the countryside. The Haitians describe a zombie as an animated corpse that has returned to the land of the living, through the mysterious or mystic means of sorcery or witchcraft. Quite often there will be one zombie prowling through a village or town, instead of a group of zombies destroying life as we know it.

In Haiti, the term that they use to describe is 'zonbi', and in North Mbundu it's 'nzumbe', both close to the English version, zombie.

According to their beliefs, the deceased person could be revived and brought back to life by a Bokor, which means sorcerer. Once the deceased person has been brought back or reanimated, they are then under the control of the Bokor who brought them back. Until they are killed again, or released by the Bokor, they are destined to walk the land of the living in a deathlike state. They are neither alive or dead, simply lingering among the living.

There is an explanation for this phenomenon, other than mystical powers of being able to revive the dead. During the 1980s a Harvard Ethnobotanist, Wade Davis, traveled to Haiti to investigate and learn as much as possible about zombies and zombie powder. What he discovered was that the Bokor administered a powder that placed the person in a state close to death. With the burials occurring relatively quickly, normally within 24 hours of death, the person then awakened. More often than not the person who had been given the zombie powder died of suffocation, due to a lack of oxygen when they were buried.

Although the different Bokors used slightly different methods and variations, Davis discovered that there were several consistent ingredients:

- Burned and then ground-up human bones or remains.
- A variety of small tree frog.
- The Polychate worm.
- A large New World toad.
- One of the many different varieties of puffer fish.

Out of all of these different ingredients in the zombie powder, the pufferfish is the single most important one. Pufferfish contain a deadly nerve toxin that is known as Tetrodotoxin. In smaller amounts, the poison of the pufferfish leaves your arms and legs tingling, with a feeling of euphoria. When larger doses are consumed, it can cause death within minutes. The zombie powder contains a level of the Tetrodotoxin slightly below lethal, leaving its victims' breathing subdued, and a heart rate of almost zero, suspended animation at its finest.

All going well, the Bokor has managed to poison his victim and fooled friends and family into believing that they're dead. After they're buried, the Bokor normally returns to the burial ground and attempts to dig up the body, and with any luck they haven't suffocated. The Bokor then administers a second drug, a psychoactive drug that is made of Jimson weed. The zombie is now suffering from delirium and disorientation, leaving them under the control of the Bokor.

The Bokor now has a perfect slave, and often the whole process was undertaken to reconfirm the Bokor's powers. There are also other reasons why a Bokor may turn someone into a zombie, such as revenge, power, extortion and even experimentation. This isn't something that is a remnant of the past either; this is still continuing in many places today.

## *Part 2 – Chemical Zombies*

At this point, the facts or fiction surrounding secret government experiments involving the dead and reanimation can neither be confirmed or denied. Have they done it? Maybe, probably, who really knows? It's not like the government hasn't done some very, very questionable things over the years, and then either lied to us or covered them up. By our very nature, humans are very curious creatures indeed. They say that curiosity killed the cat; well, it has also killed quite a few humans over the years and will most likely continue to do so.

As a prime example of this we have the experiment conducted by the CIA during the height of the Cold War, between the USSR and the United States of America. For over two decades, the CIA spent over $20 million dollars conducting experiments on subjects without their knowledge or consent. The CIA subjected these people to things such as experimental drugs, LSD and barbiturates, hypnosis, and even radiological and biological agents, it's been reported. It's alleged that the end goal of their experiments was to control the minds of people, and then use them for either willing or unwilling assassinations. It isn't that much of a stretch, therefore, to imagine them accidentally creating a swarm of zombies.

It could be an accident involving the mixing of chemicals that results in zombies swarming the land, or it could be scientists experimenting with bringing back the dead. These chemical zombies vary significantly from a television show or movie; indeed, they are a different breed of zombies altogether. Yet there are certain things that all the so-called zombie experts agree on, such as that they will be faster, smarter and have more control than your average zombie.

Chemical zombies may not always be able to infect their victims through a bite or scratch like other zombies, but there are other ways that you might contract the sickness. It could be contracted through the ingestion of contaminated meat, inhaling the chemicals that were originally involved, or through airborne contact. Some of the signs that you may have contracted the affliction of the chemical zombie are chills, coughs, tightness of limbs and joints, respiratory issues, irregular heartbeats, rigor mortis, and then eventual total control of your mind and functions.

The remains of the chemical zombie should be treated with the maximum amount of care possible. The flesh and the blood of the chemical zombie, and even the ashes of a burned zombie could contaminate a large area. Even now there is no exact science to getting rid of the highly contagious remains of a chemical zombie, so until there is, the bodies must be securely sealed in air-tight biohazard body bags. After they have been bagged, the bodies should then be stored in a secure freezing facility.

These zombies are probably the type we have the highest chance of facing. To kill them you should sever the brain and brain stem while being extremely careful not to become contaminated yourself.

## *Part 3 – Parasitic Zombies*

Considered possibly one of the scariest zombies out there, the parasitic zombie is really too frightening to consider. These zombies are created when a host organism such as an animal or a human being is invaded by an extremely sophisticated parasitic organism.

So far as I know, writing this book, there are no known parasites that have exhibited the abilities to work under the system of a hive-mind. That could change at any moment; every day new animals, insects and parasites are being discovered, and zombies could be walking around the perimeter of my premises as I type.

Parasitic zombies normally operate in an extremely connected and overly aggressive hive-mind situation. They are fast, agile, aggressive and work extremely well together.

As far as can be established, parasitic zombies show a wide range of symptoms before changing, such as:

- Aggression
- Schizophrenia
- Confusion
- Loss of memory
- Blindness
- Neurological damage
- Diarrhea
- Physical discomfort & joint pain
- Vomiting & nausea
- Thirst for human flesh

Narrowing down exactly how to treat the parasite infecting the host can be extremely hard, but not impossible. The problem will be how much time you will have to wait for a successful antibiotic to be developed. In the meantime, there are other ways to destroy the parasite, but these are usually invasive and cause the host to die as well.

The parasite can live in any number of places and environments. These could be things like mud, water, feces, blood, flesh, food, etc.; the list goes on and on. Most parasitic zombie outbreaks start in places where there are poor living conditions, poor water and sanitation, and inadequate medical facilities. Parasites are driven to do only two things: reproduce and survive. Their sole goal is to find a compatible host, ensure their survival and then reproduce to ensure their continuance. This means that you now have lethal zombies, driven to kill and eat, spreading the host-parasite as far and as wide as they possibly can.

One disadvantage that a parasitic zombie may have over other zombies is in its drive to survive. This is because the host is always looking for the optimum living conditions to ensure its survival. You could be considerably safer in environments of extreme heat or cold, where the host-parasite is at a distinct disadvantage. This is a prime example of the parasitic zombie nature being used against it as a weapon to control its spread. Remember, everything in nature adapts, and parasites are no different. This strategy could work well in the beginning, but as hosts and food for the parasite become scarcer then it may very well adapt and move into these areas. This wouldn't happen at the start, but most likely towards the end of an outbreak.

Much like other zombies, parasitic zombies will prove to be extremely difficult to kill. After the host, or zombie, has sustained enough damage the parasite will need to get a new host. Once dead, the parasite will attempt to seek out a new host as soon as possible before it dies itself. Always take every precaution when disposing of the remains.

## *Part 4 – Viral Zombies*

For as long as man has walked the earth, there have been viruses walking hand in hand with him. Some people claim that it wasn't an asteroid that caused the dinosaur's extinction, it was a virus. Viruses have been killing animals and humans for thousands of years; they are nature's way of leveling the playing field. Before I get into viral zombies, I will briefly cover the top five viruses, what they are and what they do. This is just to give us an idea of what a virus could do, let alone a viral zombie.

- **Marburg Virus** – The Marburg virus was first identified by scientists in 1967 when lab workers in Germany were exposed to infected monkeys from Uganda. It's very similar to the Ebola virus; it causes hemorrhagic fever, which means that the people who are infected develop high fevers and bleeding throughout the body, which eventually leads to organ failure and death. The mortality rate during the first outbreak was 25%; in the latest outbreak in the Congo it was closer to 80%.

- **Ebola Virus** – Ebola was first recorded in humans during outbreaks in both the Sudan and the Democratic Republic of Congo in 1976. It is spread through contact with bodily fluids such as vomit, feces, blood, etc. There is a variety of different strains, and they vary quite substantially from strain to strain. The mortality rate can be as low as 25% but can climb to 80% for some strains.

- **Rabies** – The rabies threat for most countries is almost non-existent due to vaccines. However, in many parts of India and Africa it is still considered a big problem. It attacks the brain of the victim, sending them crazy. If you were bitten by a rabid animal and contracted the disease, left untreated, it would certainly kill you.

- **HIV** – One of the deadliest viruses facing the entire world could very well be HIV. It has been estimated that HIV is responsible for the deaths of over 36 million people since it was first recognized in the 1980s. There are extremely powerful antiviral drugs available that help to alleviate some effects of the disease, but these are almost impossible to obtain for low-income countries. Also sub-Saharan Africa accounts for two-thirds of the global total of new HIV infections[1].

- **Smallpox** – The world was declared free of smallpox in 1980 by the World Health Assembly. Before this, humans fought against smallpox for thousands of years. Smallpox has a mortality rate of approximately 35%. Where the virus was introduced outside of Europe, that hadn't built up natural immunity, the mortality rate was as high as 90%. It has been estimated that smallpox killed over 300 million people in the 20th century alone.

So that's a small taste of some of the biggest and worst viruses on the planet. Consider that the next time you hear people complaining about vaccinations. Without the rigorous vaccination program to get rid of smallpox, we would still be battling it today.

Is it that much of a stretch then to think that one of these viruses, which have been around for thousands of years, constantly changing and evolving, could mutate and unleash a wave of viral zombies? Nope, not much of a stretch at all when you consider it. It might not be a man that makes the fatal connection, it could be nature alone; viruses could mutate and evolve into a super virus. Although, when you think of some of the hideous things that man has made, it's highly likely that it will be a scientist in a lab somewhere. I'm sure they all have only the best intentions, but accidents do happen. I'm sure I wouldn't want to be the guy or girl trying to explain that accident.

Think about this; the following are a list of things that man has either created by accident or on purpose:

- **Mustard Gas** – As if being smashed by some of the heaviest explosives ever used wasn't enough, the Germans invented mustard gas during World War 1 to gas allied troops in the trenches. It was named mustard gas because of its yellow/brown color.

- **Sarin** – Was developed during World War 2. I know right, another great invention inspired by war. Sarin is listed as part of the Killer B's. Its symptoms are listed by the acronym SLUDGE - Salivation, Lacrimation, Urination, Defecation, Gastrointestinal Distress and Emesis. Sounds neat, huh?

- **VX** – Be proud the United Kingdom! You invented possibly one of the world's deadliest nerve agents, possibly up to 10 times as deadly as Sarin. VX was that pretty green stuff in the popular movie "The Rock", and is code named "Purple Possum." Luckily it has been banned since 1993, and most countries have destroyed their stockpiles.

Nice, right? So is it really that hard to imagine that a laboratory accident somewhere could unleash a virus, infecting man and turning us all into zombies? No, it's not. That's the scary part. There isn't a lot that we can do as individuals to prevent that from happening, but we can be as prepared as possible.

Your typical viral zombie is only driven by one main impulse, and that is to feed. By feeding it spreads the virus to new hosts, maintaining its lifespan. Depending on the type of viral infection, viral zombies could either be quite slow or amazingly quick. Depending on the amount of damage that the brain has received, a viral zombie could show some signs of intelligence and memory retention.

Viral zombies don't need to rest, eat, or sleep. When they are feeding on their victims, it isn't for nutrition, it's simply to spread the virus to new victims, giving the virus a new host. They are a relentless enemy; they will pursue their victims through all manner of obstacles, only stopping when they are too damaged to move, or they're destroyed. They don't feel pain like a normal person, and would continue to pursue their victims even if they had nothing left below their necks.

You could handle a slow-moving zombie quite easily yourself, but once they start to group up, even the handiest fighter could become overwhelmed. Faster viral zombies should be treated with as much caution as possible; being able to close to within striking distance is quite easy for viral zombies. They don't feel pain so will be relentless in their attack.

Bites, scratches or even being exposed to the fluids of viral zombies can be enough to infect you, so take all precautions possible when dispatching viral zombies or destroying their remains. Some common symptoms of infection are fever, blurred vision, weakness in the limbs, joint pains, graying skin, disorientation and eventually a coma, death and the inevitable reanimation. This could all happen as quickly as an hour, or a week; it all depends on the severity of the infection.

Try to remember that beneath the viral infection, the viral zombie is still a human being, and as such shouldn't be killed unless all other avenues are exhausted. Scientists could discover an immunization or cure that could restore zombies back to their normal condition.

So there we have four of the main types of zombies that you will most likely encounter. Each of these main four types of zombies will have slightly different variations, but generally they will exhibit the same characteristics. Remember to be as careful as possible when you are handling the remains of destroyed zombies, no matter what type they are. Also, try to remember that all of these zombies at one point were human beings, just like you and I.

## Chapter Two

# STAYING PUT OR KEEPING MOBILE

### *Part 1. Staying Put*

So the worst has happened. Swarms of zombies are moving across the countryside killing anything that they come across. Let's assume that you have decided to batten down the hatches and stick it out in your home or business. It's not just a matter of locking a few doors or windows either; you have a whole hell of a lot of planning and preparation to do - if you have the time, that is. In the following chapter I'll try to go into as much detail as possible, as the more prepared you are, the longer you'll survive. Remember that it might not always be possible for you to stay and wait it out. You might be waiting hours, days, weeks, months or even years, if help comes at all. If the zombie outbreak is worldwide then there may not be any help coming; if it's more localized or contained to one country, it could take months for a rescue force to be organized.

It doesn't matter if you are defending a caravan or a mansion, it's still your home, and you have a certain home ground advantage by staying in one place. You can't just lock your doors and hope no one notices you. It could be the living dead, or it could be other people looking to take advantage of those weaker than them. If you know your area well, you'll have an advantage over other people who might be unfamiliar with the surroundings.

It will take a lot of work to get your safe house or bunker ready, and you may not have enough time. If you are already prepared for an end-of-the-world situation, you'll have a distinct advantage over your enemies.

## *Step One. Security*

Secure your location. This is probably one of the most important steps to take. You can always get more supplies by venturing outside, but if you can't defend the location, you're already dead. Remember, if you're securing it from the outside only, people could always undo all of your hard work. The ideal situation is to secure it from the inside, making the outside seem as normal as possible. Even better would be making the outside look deserted and not worth a second glance. If a location looks as if it has nothing of value and has already been searched, people will be less likely to bother searching it again.

Board up, block and lock all doors and windows on the ground floor that lead to the outside. This will be the main access point for any intruders, so spend as much time as possible making this area secure. If you can secure a door from the outside, yet leave it easily disabled from the inside, you have a possible emergency exit point. Just remember that if it's easier to get out of, it could be easier to get into from the outside.

Below is a relatively secure and easy way to secure your doors against intruders.

With the exterior doors secured, the next thing is to secure the windows. Unfortunately, you probably won't have time to install metal security bars or grills, so you have to deal with the windows as best you can. If you happen to have sheets of thick marine ply or other sheeting close by that would be perfect. However, we don't always have lumber ready and standing by to secure our premises so you may have to make do with what you can. Any tables, benches or shelves are great places to start. Next you have all internal doors and cupboard doors. Just make sure you use the strongest items; internal doors may appear strong, but are often quite flimsy compared to say a slightly thinner cupboard or wardrobe door.

A handy tip here. If you have room in an attic or basement, sheets of strong ply when stacked correctly take up very little space. A dozen sheets of ply or concrete sheeting and an equal amount of 2x4s will be invaluable in any disaster, be it apocalyptic or natural disaster.

Securing all of this with nails will do if that's all that you have, but screws are preferable for long-term strength and durability. A box of 1000 nails or screws won't cost much and take up very little space, but could save your life. A set of screwdrivers, hammers, pry bars or crowbars would serve you quite well, and should be stored along with the building materials. Try to stay away from cheap materials like particle boards as they will deteriorate quickly, especially if they're exposed to the weather.

Once your main entry points at ground level are secured, it's time to move on and focus on the upper and lower levels. If your basement has windows, you will need to secure them. This could be done by blocking them from the inside, then backfilling them from the outside. You'll be surprised at how quickly nature will cover up your recent earthworks. Basements can make great bolt holes if you think that you have lost control over the upper levels of the house. Depending on how much time you have, you could even construct emergency tunnel exits out of your basement into other dwellings or surroundings. Board up all your upper windows, and if you have exterior fire escapes or landings it would be better to dismantle them if you can't bring them up to the upper level. It's hard to focus on defending the ground floor, basement and upper floors all at once.

Okay, we have all access points secured and under our control. The less access points you have, the easier your building will be to defend. You need to get into the routine of regularly checking that all your security is still secure and if possible upgraded. This should be the first thing you do when you rise in the morning, and the last thing you do before you sleep at night. After all, what else have you got to do anyway? It's not like you're missing a game.

## *Step Two. Stock Take*

Now that you have your location as secure as possible it's time to go through everything that you have and work out what you need. If you have already prepared an Emergency Kit (please refer to Chapter Three) or Bug-Out Bag (B.O.B), it's time to grab it out and work out exactly what you have in it. You need to work out exactly what you have, how much of it, and then get it as organized as possible. It's not much use having a torch and a supply of batteries if the torch is in a drawer upstairs and the batteries are locked in a cupboard in the basement.

Below is a guide on how to organize your possessions so you know exactly what you have and when they may run out.

- If you have functioning infrastructure keep your water storage filled to their maximum levels. If you have a bathtub, laundry sink, and kitchen sink then keep them topped up with fresh water. Next, fill as many containers as possible and store them in safe locations. While you're not doing much or in cooler climates you may only need approximately 1 gallon of water per person per day. If you are moving around a lot or live in a warmer climate, you may need to allow up to 2 gallons per person per day. (For advice on keeping your drinking water safe to drink, or how to purify your water, please refer to Chapter Three.)

- Sort all of your food into staples that will last. It doesn't make a lot of sense to eat all your canned goods straight away if you have other food items that will expire first. You should always plan for any help to arrive long after you expect it. Eat as little as possible to remain healthy and active. Along with food, you need to make sure you have adequate cooking utensils ready. You will need small pots and pans, utensils, plates, large spoons, etc. Remember, if you have pets, then you will need to allow for their eating and drinking needs as well. You have to weigh up whether you have enough water to wash up your utensils or if it's better to use disposable items. Trash may attract more attention that it's worth, from animals, humans and the hungry walking dead. (For more detailed advice on food preparation and storage, please refer to Chapter Three.)

- This is pretty high up there on the list of must-have things. We need it to cook our food and to provide warmth. It can also be our worst enemy if not treated with respect. If you lose control of your fire, it may just kill you quicker than the zombies ever could. When you're setting up your fire, you must have adequate ventilation. It doesn't matter if you're burning gas or wood, the fumes need to go somewhere, or you may fall asleep and never wake up. A few things that you should keep a good stock of are strike-anywhere matches, candles, butane lighters, fire strikers and tinder (shredded paper or wood shavings are good). Remember to keep your fire as small as possible, light and smoke are visible from long distances. People can see the light of your fire at night if you're not careful. They can also see the smoke easily through the day and smell it long after you put the fire out.

- You can buy medical kits online or through local stores. Another good idea is to build your own. Make sure that you keep it in a secure, safe and dry container, it could just save your life or a loved one's. Toolboxes and fishing tackle boxes make excellent storage containers for your first aid kit. It should contain roll bandages, gauze pads, medical tape, tweezers, scissors, alcohol wipes, aspirin, gloves, bandages, sanitizer, face masks, a medical guide, needles and thread, and any other item you could think of. If you could take basic first aid courses and CPR, then this would be a huge benefit to you and your family.

- Like having a good fire, just having light during the night can be an amazing advantage. Not only in being able to find items, but it can also make you feel secure and safe. You need candles, LED flashlights, oil lamps and lanterns. Keep as many batteries or lamp fuels as possible. Remember your light security; don't use lights and advertise to everybody in the neighborhood that you're inside. If possible test out your rooms individually at night, check to make sure no light is escaping and then fix it. If it's too hard to fix, then don't use lights in that particular area unless it's an emergency.

- There is always something that you will need and won't have. It's hard to be prepared for every conceivable situation or emergency, so the best we can do is be as prepared as possible. The following items will see you through most situations: small tool kit, hammer, nails, screws, hand saw, screwdrivers, tape measure, razor blades, tape, glue, pliers, wire-cutters, batteries, light bulbs, bleach, plastic bags, shovel, pick, rope, wire, extension cords and blankets. Obviously there are a million different things that you'll need, so please feel free to add as many items as you see fit.

## Step Three. Secure Your Utilities

Not every disaster will require you to do anything to secure the utilities. The electricity will be the first thing that is switched off, as it requires a lot of ongoing maintenance. Water and sewage will last longer, but eventually these too will stop working. Most natural disasters won't require you to do a lot to secure your utilities, but zombie outbreaks will require that you pay a little extra attention.

Electricity is probably the thing that we require the most, so it's ironic that it will be the first thing that disappears from our lives. If you are lucky enough to have a generator, use it as little as possible, in emergency situations where it could save your life. The noise and fumes are enough to attract the worst kind of people and zombies. You can get a hand crank or pedal power generators that are easy to maintain and will operate quietly. You can use them to charge batteries that you can use later at your convenience. Another good idea if you have them installed beforehand is solar panels. Depending on your disaster situation, you could also remove solar panels from other buildings in the area.

If you have gas lines that run directly to your house, it would be best if you shut them off where they enter the building. Bleed all the gas out of the lines inside the house a little at a time in case there is a fire or leak.

You should always consider shutting off the water if you fear that it may become contaminated. There is also the chance of flooding occurring if water was to come through the toilet or baths, etc. You could shut off the water where it enters your property or individually shut it off at certain locations through the building, toilets, sinks, bathtubs, etc.

## *Step Four. Weapons and Defense*

Now that you have secured your premises and taken stock of all of your supplies it's time to focus on weapons and defense. You should have a weapon or weapons with you or next to you, every single minute of the day; this includes while you sleep. If you're inside the house, you should have shorter weapons that you can swing freely without worrying about getting caught up in anything. Hammers, crowbars, bats or anything short yet heavy.

Firearms like pistols, shotguns and rifles work extremely well, but you have to consider the time it takes to reload and the noise that they make. All guns, even when silenced, should be considered as a last resort.

Setting up barricades inside your building is an extremely good idea. This gives you pre-prepared defense positions inside your home. Each one should be stocked with a weapon, and when you fall back, it's ready to be defended. (For more information on weapons please refer to Chapter Four.)

## *Step Five. The Miscellaneous Things*

We have covered security, supplies, utilities and defense. So what's left? Just a few smaller things that you wouldn't necessarily think of but could just save your life.

- Keep yourself active, work out every day and maintain a routine. If it gets too easy, then switch it up and push yourself.

- Keep your mind healthy by reading or doing writing exercises. Try keeping a journal or diary; it's an easy way to occupy yourself and takes up very little room or supplies.

- Keep up your morale by playing board games and cards, and tell old stories to each other.

- Keep yourself as clean as possible by maintaining regular bathing habits. Wash your hands and face as much as possible, clean your teeth, change your clothes, trim your facial hair and head hair. It's easier to keep up your spirits if you keep doing the things that keep you normal.

I wish you the best of luck if the worst is happening or happens. We all have to do what we need to do to survive; when we become animals we have already lost ourselves.

## *Part 2. Keeping Mobile*

The worst has happened. The dead have risen and are walking or running among the living. Do you run or do you stay and fight? The ultimate survivalist question. Sometimes it's better to run, while at other times it may be better to lock up tight and wait it all out. What you do will ultimately depend on your personal situation; everyone's will be different and require a different answer. Let's just say that for this section you have decided to hit the road, and you ain't never coming back, Jack.

The first thing you need to do is grab your emergency pack or Bug-Out Bag (B.O.B) and get going. (Please refer to Chapter Three to find out more about B.O.Bs.) Your B.O.B will have as much as you can comfortably carry and will be your best friend wherever you go. If you use items out of your B.O.B, try to replace them as soon as possible so that you have them ready for the next time. Try to add items that could be of use as you come across them, but be realistic, as you can't carry everything all over the countryside with you.

You have to choose how you're going to travel next. After a major disaster or zombie outbreak, the majority of roads and highways will most likely be blocked by people trying to flee. There will be other survivors using the highways that could be friendly or looking for weaker victims to prey on. Then, just to top it all off, there will be zombies because where there are a lot of people, there will also be a lot of zombies looking to kill and eat them.

If you're traveling by foot, you have a lot of options for where you can go, but you will be limited to how fast and far you can travel. It's also harder to get away quickly if you have too, but remember you may not be in a situation where you need to get away if no one notices you. You won't be able to carry as much, but a pair of boots is a hell of a lot easier to maintain than a vehicle. There are pros and cons to every situation, so you'll have to weigh each one up and evaluate your personal needs.

If you choose to use any motor vehicle, then you have a lot more options in one sense and also a lot less. Motorbikes are a decent balance between having no transport and a vehicle, as they will require less fuel but still enable you to cover a lot of territory and carry extra supplies. We'll start with the pros of motor-vehicles and then move onto the cons. (Please refer to Chapter Eight to get more information on setting up your vehicle.)

- You can cover a lot more ground when you are using a motor-vehicle.

- You will be able to move around faster and get out of a dangerous situation quicker.

- You can carry more equipment with you. This means more rations and more survival equipment.

- You have a certain amount of protection from the elements and zombies.

- Your vehicle will require regular maintenance that will be hard to come by; you can't just stop at a local garage and get a mechanic to service your car.

- Your vehicle will require fuel. As above, there probably won't be gas stations around every corner.
- Your vehicle makes a lot of noise, which can attract unwanted attention both from other people and zombies.

Now that we have decided on traveling by foot or with a vehicle, the next thing we need to talk about is having a plan of action. The best idea is to get out of the city and try to find somewhere as remote as possible. The fewer people who were there before the zombies took over, the better, as it means that there will be fewer zombies that you will have to deal with.

You'll need detailed maps and a compass. This is something that you should have prepared and placed in your B.O.B. If you can get maps printed and laminated even better, as they will be protected from damage and they'll also last longer. Work out where you're heading and pick alternate routes in case your path is blocked or something happens and you need to move quickly. You want to find somewhere that has water, plants, vegetables and game. Stay away from cities or large towns at all costs, as these places are natural gathering points for zombies and people alike.

You have to consider traveling at night as a possible choice. It will make movement through dense areas harder, and the element of surprise works both ways. People may not be able to see you, but you won't be able to see them either. If you have to travel at night, try to keep it as a last resort. No matter which way you choose to travel people may be able to see you before you see them, so make sure you are paying attention at all times. Look for signs that other people have traveled through the area recently, and signs of zombies. If you have to stop, make sure that you choose a position that is suited to defense and have your escape plan ready. Plan where you will go if you're attacked, how long it will take to get there and what you need to do to get there.

Sometimes our first instinct or our "gut" instinct is our brain telling us something isn't right, but it isn't exactly sure why. You need to learn to trust your instincts as much as possible. If you feel that something isn't right or that you could be in danger, then get out of there and move to a position that you feel is safer. Try to avoid congested areas, cities, bridges, highways, dead-end roads and tunnels.

When you enter any new area, it's imperative that you do a thorough reconnaissance. Try and avoid any school buildings, malls, government buildings and other places where people were most likely congregating before the zombie virus struck. Make sure that you look for signs of other survivors, friendly or hostile. Check for signs of battles and fires, damaged or dangerous structures. If you enter a building make sure you check all the exits; you need to know how to get out of places as fast as possible if anything goes wrong.

When you decide it's time to stop for the night, if possible stop before the sun goes down. This will give you the advantage of seeing the entire area, and not stopping in the dark next to a mall full of zombies! If you can find buildings where you can hide your vehicle and secure yourself for the night, that's even better. Make sure you check to see if other people are in the area or if they have been there recently. The place you choose to sleep the night could be some other group's safe house. If you have secured the area as much as possible try to spend the night going over your stockpile of equipment and supplies. Keep busy, but always remain vigilant.

Remember to keep moving as much as possible. Plan where you're going and be prepared for anything.

# Chapter Three

## PREPARATION & SUPPLIES

### *Part 1. Emergency Kit or Bug-Out Bag (BUB)*

Bug-Out Bags (B.O.B) or Emergency Escape Bags are always a pretty hotly debated subject among survivalists. There is a variety of different options on the market that you could purchase as a complete, ready-to-go option, but it's recommended that you create your own. The first good reason for this is that you get the option of putting exactly what you want in it. The second reason is that when it comes to an emergency situation you'll know exactly what you have, how much and where it is inside your bag. That means that you won't be searching around in the dark trying to work out where things are; you'll know what part of the bag it's in and how many of them you have.

If you're new to being a Survivalist, then creating your first B.O.B can seem like a massive undertaking and quite complicated. However, once you break it down it's really just a matter of going through your checklist and making sure you have exactly what you need, without becoming overloaded. You might not be able to have everything you will ever need in your B.O.B, but you'll definitely be a lot more prepared than someone who has done nothing.

Most people spend years building their personal B.O.Bs. They constantly get their equipment out and swap it out for new and improved gear as it becomes available. The ultimate aim for your B.O.B is to keep you going and get you far enough away from danger. Obviously you won't be able to live off your B.O.B forever, but you should have enough supplies and equipment inside to last you 72 hours. Start at sustaining yourself for a minimum of 3 days, then tweak it. See what you could do without and perhaps what extra items you could include.

You have to consider that you may not be able to get out with a vehicle, so plan on carrying your B.O.B and work out what you're comfortable with. Another thing to consider is whether you will be alone or have friends and family members with you. Everyone should be responsible for carrying their own B.O.B unless they are a small child or perhaps unwell.

Let's start with seven of the main types of equipment that you'll need in your B.O.B, and then move on from there.

## *Number One – Water*

This is probably one of the main things that you will need to have inside your B.O.B; it's also heavy and takes up a lot of room. 1 liter of water per person, per day, is recommended as the absolute minimum. While the water infrastructure remains functional, it is always recommended that you keep bottled water filled up. Your B.O.B should contain at least 3 liters of water if you plan on lasting 72 hours. You can boil water to keep it purified and use iodine tablets, or you can look at purchasing a decent water filtration system.

## *Number Two – Food*

For the food situation, there is a wide variety of backpack meals, MRE's and energy bars to get you through the first critical 72 hours. Backpack meals are freeze-dried meals that you just need to add boiling water to. They are extremely light, take up little space and will last a long time. In the end, you will need to find a more permanent solution to your food needs, but for those first few days these meals will get you out of trouble.

## *Number Three – Clothes*

You should pack enough clothes to last you at least three days. Obviously in the middle of a zombie apocalypse you aren't worried about fashion; it's practicality that matters. Pack clothes suitable for both warm and cold weather. You'll need a good pair of hiking/walking boots, a good pair of long pants, two pairs of good quality socks, two shirts (long & short sleeve), a waterproof jacket, thermal pants & top, a hat, and a bandana. You could pack more, but this should be considered a minimum for you to get by for three days.

## *Number Four – Shelter*

It doesn't matter if you have a vehicle or a place you plan on bugging out to, you should include an alternative form of shelter in your B.O.B. Depending on who you will be travelling with you'll need at least a one-man tent, and a ground tarp for underneath your tent that could also be used as an emergency shelter itself. A high-quality all-weather sleeping bag, bedroll or swag would be ideal. Try to consider the weight of whatever you may have to carry.

## *Number Five – First Aid Kit*

Okay, covering everything that you'll need in your first aid kit is almost a book by itself. I covered some of the more specific items in the previous chapter, so I won't bore you with it again. Most experts recommend that you build your first aid kit instead of buying one. They all claim to have everything you need and they just might do, but what's the point of having a snake bite kit if there are no snakes? It also means that they may have left out extra bandages to pack something else. If you build your first aid kit, you'll know exactly what's in it and where it is. I recommend doing a first aid course and CPR course. Also, consider putting a compact medical book inside your first aid kit.

## *Number Six – Basic Equipment*

This is where we will cover all of the miscellaneous items that don't need a category by themselves but are important nonetheless. Obviously you can't carry everything with you, so it will be up to personal preference what makes the final cut to your B.O.B. First you'll need rain equipment, as it's extremely important to keep yourself dry to prevent illness. Consider a camouflage poncho or thin raincoat to be worked over your jacket. Have you ever tried to start a fire with a rock in the rain? Sounds pretty damn rough. You'll want to include strike-anywhere matches, a butane lighter and ordinary matches. Something that might seem obvious at the time, when you're sitting looking at a fire with food in the other hand and no pot, you'll need a pan or pot to cook meals on and to boil water. Consider adding a small camping stove with its own fuel source that fits inside the pot you choose. You'll also want two ultimate light sources. Small LED flashlights use little battery power so will last you quite a while and won't take up much space. Consider spending a little bit more on your torch and getting a high-quality waterproof and shockproof model. Lastly, get a high-quality, multi-purpose survival knife. This will definitely need a lot more of a detailed explanation, and I will cover that in the weapons section.

## *Number Seven – Weapons*

In a zombie apocalypse, you will need a weapon for protection against not only zombies but also against other people looking to take whatever you have. There will most likely be a complete breakdown of law and order, so your own protection is extremely important. I'm not going into much detail about weapons here as I will be covering it in much more depth later on.

A pistol is probably one of the most versatile weapons that you could have in your B.O.B. It's small, light, and you'll be able to carry extra ammunition in magazines ready to go, depending on what sort of pistol you choose. You could choose to carry a rifle or also a shotgun. Whatever you choose will be more of a personal choice as each firearm will be good for different situations.

If you don't want to use a firearm, there are some other good choices for you as well. You could choose a high-power sling shot with ball bearings. A crossbow or bow is also another good choice for hunting and defense. Bats, clubs or knives are also good, especially if it's a last-minute addition as you leave the house. Finally, if you like, you could choose to take a multi-purpose combat axe or hammer. These are ideal for close combat self-defense, as well as chopping wood, building defensive positions and general duties.

Another extremely good idea to do is make a smaller pack with enough items to get you through approximately 12-24 hours. This should be attached to you separately to your main B.O.B. This way, if anything was to happen where you had to get out quickly, you could drop the main B.O.B but still have some equipment left over.

I'm going to include a detailed checklist below of everything your B.O.B could include. This can be a great way to make sure that you have everything you need and will also help remind you of some other gear that you might not have considered.

## *B.O.B Equipment Checklist*

### Water

- ☐ Water For Up To 72 Hours
- ☐ Water Containers
- ☐ Hydration Bladders
- ☐ Filtration Kit

### Food

- ☐ Ration Packs / MRE's
- ☐ Energy Bars
- ☐ Powder Energy Drinks
- ☐ Vitamins / Supplements

- ☐ Can Opener
- ☐ Cooking Pot / Pan
- ☐ Utensils

## Clothes

- ☐ 1 Pair Long Pants
- ☐ 2 Long & Short Sleeve Shirts
- ☐ 2 Socks & Underwear
- ☐ Thermal Pants & Top
- ☐ Waterproof Jacket
- ☐ Raincoat
- ☐ Sturdy and Comfortable Hiking Boots
- ☐ Hat
- ☐ Bandana
- ☐ Baklava
- ☐ Gloves

## Shelter

- ☐ Tent
- ☐ Ground Tarp
- ☐ Sleeping Bag
- ☐ Swag
- ☐ Extra Thermal Blankets

## First Aid Kit

- ☐ Antibiotics
- ☐ Gauze
- ☐ Bandages
- ☐ Gloves
- ☐ Tape
- ☐ Medication
- ☐ Headache Tablets
- ☐ Sterilizer
- ☐ Sling
- ☐ Tweezers
- ☐ Scalpel
- ☐ Super Glue
- ☐ Triangle Bandage

## Basic Equipment

- ☐ Strike-Anywhere Matches
- ☐ Butane Lighters
- ☐ Camping Stove
- ☐ LED Flashlights
- ☐ Spare Batteries
- ☐ Map & Compass
- ☐ Duct Tape
- ☐ Signal Mirror
- ☐ Hygiene Kit

- ☐ Insect Repellent
- ☐ Para Cord or Rope
- ☐ Head Lamp
- ☐ Fishing Kit
- ☐ Dusk Masks
- ☐ Tools, Screwdrivers, Wrench, Hammer, Saw.

**Weapons**

- ☐ Pistol, Rifle or Shotgun
- ☐ Slingshot
- ☐ Crossbow
- ☐ Ammunition
- ☐ Spare Parts
- ☐ Combat Knife
- ☐ Combat Hammer
- ☐ Combat Shovel

## *Part 2. Water Filtration & Purification*

It's easy to take something that is available 24/7 for granted. Everywhere we go we can drink out of a tap, water fountain or just stop and buy a bottle of water. During a zombie apocalypse, the utilities would soon be non-existent. Without people to operate them, electricity, gas, water and sewerage would soon shut down. Water may continue to work slightly longer than the electricity or gas but once it turns off, you will lose sewage as well. Sewage could become backed up or flood, and then contaminate local water sources. Often, during floods the water level rises and quickly makes any water contaminated.

At a minimum, we need at least a gallon of water per person per day, for drinking, hygiene, and food preparation. You could go into local areas and scavenge bottled water, but this exposes you to other dangers. Other people could be in the area looking for the same thing, and the more populated the area, the more zombies will be around. Depending on how long the emergency situation lasts, there won't be bottled water around forever. It doesn't matter if you settle down in one particular area or stay on the move, you'll need to come up with a way to have safe drinking water.

On average, depending on the temperature and what sort of activity you're up to, a person could last approximately three days without water. Once dehydration and malnutrition set in your chances of survival will be considerably lowered. Remember, it only takes 24 hours for the first signs of dehydration to set in.

The first thing that you'll need to do is locate a source of water. Running water from a stream or river is ideal. If it's a large body of water like a lake that isn't too bad either. Small ponds or dams that contain stagnant or still water would probably be a last resort, but in the end water is water. Having detailed maps with water sources is ideal. Spend some time planning your escape routes or travel routes. Knowing where you're going and if there is water there will mean you're already one step ahead.

Don't wait a day until you're already thirsty to start sorting out your water needs either. If you have 2 or 3 days' water, then you have the perfect chance to get ahead and take care of your water needs for another couple of days. Being proactive means that if anything happens, zombies, other humans or bad weather, you'll have water in reserve.

The ideal way for you to store your water or transport would be in a strong, secure container such as a water bladder, metal water container or plastic bottle/jug. If you don't have these, you could fold a plastic sheet into the shape of a bag or line a bucket with it. Another handy way to carry water is inside a non-lubricated condom. They are light and take up very little space in your pack. Place the condom inside a sock or two socks and it will be even more secure.

Some canteens that you can purchase contain built-in screens that will prevent large particles from entering them. If you have a lot of heavy sediment in your water bottle, it will make the purification process harder, and in some cases simply ruin your filters. A cheap alternative to heavy sediment filters is coffee filters or a piece of cloth that you can keep folded away inside your pack. Your bandana is another handy piece of equipment for filtering out particles, or in a pinch you can soak water into it and squeeze it out into a container. If you have to get water from a still source, then try to find somewhere where the sediment has settled.

The difference between water filtration and purification is purified water is safe to drink but may not look the most appetizing, and filtration is what occurs before and after the purification process. You try to filter out as much dirt, leaves and crud as possible before you start the purification process. Once the water is purified it's safe to drink, though it may look like mud. We are all used to crystal-clear water, so drinking something that looks like dirty muddy water with crap floating in it is hard for some people.

It isn't a complicated process to filter your water and just achieving the basic amount of filtration is a relatively simple operation. As we mentioned above, a coffee filter or cloth folded over itself will remove a lot of the debris from your water. If you need to filter a lot of water for more than yourself or you plan on setting up a more permanent camp, then a more sophisticated filtration method will be needed.

If you choose to purchase a filtration system from a manufacturer, then you will achieve an extremely high level of filtration depending on what you're willing to spend. Some of the higher-quality filters will even filter out bacteria and most viruses.

Something else that you can consider is a personal filtration or purification straw. This is a relatively small and light item that can be carried on your person. You could include several of these into your B.O.B. Some of these straws filter anywhere from 75 liters all the way up to approximately 1,000 liters. Another variation of the straw system is a personal water bottle with a built-in filtering system. Some of these personal water bottles come with tap attachments for floods or other emergency situations. They work by just filling them up from the water source, screwing the cap on and drinking through the mouthpiece.

Remember that not all filtration systems will filter out all possible contaminants, so careful attention needs to be paid to what is contaminating the water and what you could be dealing with.

Let's move onto some different methods of purification now.

Boiling is probably one of the most well-known and easiest ways to accomplish methods of purification. Boiling water takes it above 100.C and above the virus or bacteria's heat range. Boiling water doesn't however remove harmful metals from water or dangerous chemicals that could be contaminating it.

The first step is gathering the water and running it through a simple filtration process to remove the larger debris from it. Build a fire, but remember that light and smoke may attract unwanted attention, so choose where and when you build your fire carefully. Bring a pot or metal container of water to the boil, leave it boiling for a few minutes and then let it cool.

Another option that you could consider, especially if you are set up in a position for a long amount of time, is distillation. The advantage to this method is it will also allow you to treat salt water and make it safe to drink. The water is boiled, and the steam from this boiling water is collected and retained. You can also purchase hand crank distillation systems, electrical models or solar models.

Next, let's talk about chemical treatments that we can use to treat our water. Some of the more common chemicals used to treat water are iodine, sodium chlorite / chlorine dioxide, and Chlor-Floc. There are a couple of drawbacks to these methods. You have to be able to work out dosages of chemicals and the amount of water you are treating. Some parasites may not be killed using this method and tablets can become less effective because of damage or expired chemicals. I'll talk briefly about each of the chemicals, and if you plan on using them, I recommend doing thorough research on them before use.

Iodine works by upsetting the ion balance within the cells of the bacteria, replacing the chemicals that the bacteria needs to survive. Iodine over extended periods can become harmful to humans so it shouldn't be used as a permanent solution, only a temporary one. Try not to use too much of the iodine in the water that you're treating. Some systems that you purchase come with a measured container that you simply fill up, add the appropriate amount of iodine crystals or tablets to and then shake. After you mix the iodine into your water container, it's recommended that you allow the water to rest for a minimum of 30 minutes before you drink, allowing the chemicals to mix thoroughly.

Sodium chlorite or chlorine dioxide tablets work by using chlorination as the primary source for purification. Chlorination is widely used around the world to treat large amounts of water. It works by attacking the cell walls of the bacteria or virus and killing the organism. The tablets are relatively harmless to humans and come in foil-sealed packets that are light and easy to carry, providing a handy alternative to water systems. Follow the directions on the packet, adding it to your water, shaking and allowing it to stand for several hours before drinking.

There are several sources that say that Chlor-Floc tablets aren't as reliable as the other chemical means of purification. These should probably be used as a last resort if all other options have been exhausted. In an emergency, you could use regular household bleach or regular iodine from a medical cabinet.

If you think that rescue within a certain time is imminent, you could risk drinking untreated water. This would be a last resort if all other methods of purification were exhausted. Getting sick from a viral or bacterial infection and hoping you're rescued before you become too ill is definitely not on my list of recommended activities.

## *Part 3. Food Preparation & Storage*

Preparing your Meals Ready to Eat or MRE's can be quite useful in any sort of zombie apocalypse situation. It doesn't just have to be for a zombie attack either; you could take them camping or for any sort of natural disaster. You can buy them premade, or you could make your own. The problem with the ones that are already made is that you don't know what's in them, and some of them taste like shit. You could experiment with these by adding herbs and spices, hot sauces, etc. until you're happy, or you could just make your own.

One of the biggest issues you'll face during a zombie apocalypse or any other type of natural disaster is a lack of food. It's heavy, it's bulky and it will eventually expire and be unfit to eat depending on how it's stored.

There are certain things that you want to consider when you make your own MRE. Try to choose ingredients that have a long shelf life. You can't go wrong with any sort of freeze-dried food. The lighter, the better. Remember, if you're on foot or have to fit these in your B.O.B then you don't want to be carrying around a lot of weight. You can choose to buy foods that are already dehydrated, or you can buy your own affordable dehydrator and do it yourself. Just a little note here - you can get solar powered dehydrators that could come in handy if you are going to be staying in one place for any particular length of time. You want to include foods that are high in calories. Even if you're rationing your food this way, you will at least guarantee that you are getting the most energy possible. Try to make every MRE at least a minimum of 1,200 calories. This way if you're camping, running or just surviving you will be getting the maximum amount of energy.

Here are some good ideas based on standard military MRE's:

- Breakfast: Powdered Eggs, Breakfast Bars or Dried Fruit and Nuts.

- Main Course / Entrée: Spaghetti, Beef Stews, Rice Dishes, Curries and Canned Tuna.

- Desserts: Rice Pudding, Fruit Cakes and Pound Cakes.

- Snacks / Side Dishes: Trail Mix, Dried Fruits, Jelly, Chocolate, Cookies, Mashed Potatoes, Candy, Breakfast Bars, Beef Jerky, Peanut Butter.

- Drinks: Gatorade, Powerade, Coffee, Tea, Cocoa, Shakes.

Try to avoid packing any sort of carbonated energy drinks. These are high in salt, sugar and caffeine that will ultimately leave you drinking more water and becoming possibly dehydrated.

Remember that you will need to include some way to heat your MREs unless you fancy eating them cold. Sauces, salt & pepper, bouillon cubes, soup mixes, noodles, spoons, knives & forks, and plates, etc.

are all essential items to include. You don't have to put them in every MRE but include them in your bag.

Any sort of pre-packaged, canned items like chicken, beef, tuna, anchovies, spam or instant oatmeal are great substitutes.

There are heaps of different ideas when it comes down to packaging your MRE. You are trying to aim for the least amount of packaging with the best chance of keeping your MREs protected from damage. You could use any sort of zip-type plastic bag or even better, vacuum seal them to remove air and prolong their shelf life even more.

Not all of these MREs will be instantly ready to eat, but with just a small amount of water most will be ready to go. If you pack tinned items, try and use only the cans that include a ring pull otherwise you will need to pack a can opener.

## Chapter Four

# PREFERRED ZOMBIE & DEFENSE WEAPONS

When you are in a close-combat situation, there are more considerations than a normal melee type situation. You have to consider fluids, bites, scratches, and finishing it quickly and quietly before more zombies show up. You have to fight with one eye on your surroundings, being careful that you're not being overwhelmed or becoming trapped or cornered. The longer you continue the fight, the more chance you have of becoming contaminated or wounded.

All care should be taken to avoid close-quarters combat with zombies. If you can avoid fighting them all together, that's even better. No one ever got bitten or scratched from a zombie when they were miles away from them. If there is the chance that you could slip away without a fight, that would be in your best interests. It isn't worth the risk of contamination or becoming wounded if you don't have to.

If all options of running, hiding or avoidance are exhausted, then you will have to pick up a weapon and be prepared to defend yourself and your loved ones.

## *Killing the Walking Dead*

Try to destroy the brain or sever the brain stem as quickly as possible in any fight. It looks easy but is surprisingly hard; humans have pretty damn hard heads and splitting them open isn't as easy as it looks. Try to aim for the temple, neck or the back of the neck.

If you prefer, you can also slow down the zombie before trying to finish it off. Be aware that a slow zombie is still potentially dangerous, and only fools rush in. You can aim to sever legs at the knees or the spine to slow them down, giving you the opportunity to either finish them off or flee safely. Remember that the zombie is still capable of killing even when wounded, so you could be leaving it for someone else to deal with.

The Attributes of the Perfect Zombie Weapon

- It needs to be quick and kill cleanly.
- You want to stay as far away from the zombie as possible.
- The perfect zombie weapon will last a long time.
- Multifunctional weapons like battle axes or shovels that can be used for other purposes are even better.
- Little to no maintenance is preferable.
- The least amount of training. There probably won't be schools during an apocalypse.

## *Melee or Close Combat Weapons*

I'll start with close-combat weapons or melee weapons. I'll try to cover a few different things but remember that there are hundreds of different items that can be turned into effective melee weapons with little or no effort required. Melee weapons are perfect when it becomes a face-to-face fight, in any urban combat, or when you're trying to maintain stealth and cover.

I'm not going to recommend any particular models of any of these weapons; I'll leave that up to your own personal budget and preference.

Remember, if you're not the strongest, getting a hammer that weighs too much will become more of a hindrance than a help to you in any sort of prolonged fight-or-flight situation.

## *Baseball Bat*

They will be easy to find and replace if damaged or lost. Very common, but not always the greatest when fighting zombies. Against a normal person, you will definitely be able to inflict some damage but remember zombies don't feel pain. It could take a lot of force to bash in a zombie's skull with a bat, but it may buy you extra time to make your escape.

## *Machete*

Most small knives or bladed types of weapons will be almost useless in any sort of zombie fight. If you're close enough to stab a zombie in the head or neck, you are already way too close for comfort. I would consider a knife as a last resort self-defense weapon. However, machetes or swords are a different beast altogether when it comes to killing zombies. It doesn't take a lot of training to pick one up and efficiently kill or maim a zombie. You can also use it for the construction of defenses. There is a wide variety of different types of machetes available. Swords won't be as easy to come by, and you have to make sure that it's an actual fighting sword, not just a decorative display model that is poor quality and has no edge.

## *Hammers*

They can be a deadly weapon when used to crush the skull of a zombie, but their limited reach is a major drawback. Another plus to hammers is that almost every home has one. You can get different weighted varieties with longer handles, but remember that the heavier it is, the less time you'll be able to swing it effectively for.

## *Crowbar or Pinchbar*

There are a lot of different varieties of crowbars available. You can choose a pretty standard one all the way to professional demolition models. They will be easy to come across and easy to replace if you have to leave it in a hurry. There are some titanium models available that will make them lighter than traditional steel and easier to swing around. Be careful of the reach of your crowbar, as you'll have to get relatively close.

## *Hatchets / Axes / Multi-tools*

Great for killing zombies, smashing skulls or severing spinal cords, an axe could be a deadly weapon in the right hands. Apart from the obvious uses it also makes a great tool for general use around your base or camp. You can use it to build defenses or smash your way into structures; simply put, everyone should have one.

## *DIY Zombie Weapons*

Anything that you can make or construct to suit your own specifications is probably one of the best weapons that you could possess. If you make it out of commonly found materials it will be easily replaced in the event you either lose it or you have to abandon it. You could construct this to be assembled or disassembled and placed inside your B.O.B. Remember though, it won't do you any good in an emergency if it's inside your bag.

## *Firearms*

I could write an entire book just about the different firearms that you could use to fight off zombie packs, but I'm not going to. There are thousands of different weapons to choose from, and everyone will have their own reasons for what they choose to use and why.

If you aren't trained in how to properly maintain and use a firearm, they could be less help than you think. They require ammunition and the proper care and attention. You can't just pick up a machine gun and start mowing down fields of zombies Rambo style without training.

Without adequate training, you could not only manage to shoot yourself or other people around you, but you could attract even more attention to yourself, bringing in more zombies or other people. There are many different types of silencers available on the market to suit almost every firearm, but unless you have your own they could be hard to come by.

## *Pistols*

A short gun or pistol is probably the best option for self-defense. In a pinch, this will get you out of a jam, but this isn't the movies and effectively shooting a zombie in the head isn't as easy as they make it look. There isn't a classic 'hold the pistol sideways kill shot' or magic trick that lets you get head shots one after another. You have to be able to shoot accurately, stay calm, count your shots, reload, and if all that fails get the hell out of there.

## *Rifles & Shotguns*

There are several long guns available to choose from that each have their own advantages and disadvantages. Range, noise, and the speed of reloading all have to be taken into consideration. Maintenance and ammunition are also very important to consider. It's not a lot of good if you have the perfect weapon, but it takes hard-to-find ammunition. Also, if you're using automatic rifles or shotguns you have to pay close attention to their maintenance or they will be likely to break down and jam at the worst time.

Rifles give you an excellent range advantage over most conventional shotguns but also are harder to use in any sort of urban house environment.

A shotgun is probably one of the most effective ways to clear a path inside a house situation. They inflict a serious amount of damage depending on what ammunition you use in them.

You have to be aware of the noise you're making and the unwanted attention that it will bring to you. Always maintain your weapons and be aware of your ammunition.

## *Crossbow or Other Bows*

They look really cool and badass, but are they practical? To someone who has training or the time to train then they could be the best weapon you have. However, if you just pick one up they won't be much good to you unless you have natural abilities. Remember, if you shoot a zombie with an arrow it will just keep coming unless you manage to pin it to something. The same rules apply, aim for the brain or brain stem to kill the zombie safely. Crossbows are relatively easy to maintain, depending on the model, and if you can collect the ammunition, you'll never run out. They're also silent, which makes them perfect for stealth kills and keeping out of close range.

## *Flash, Fire & Explosions*

Burning, blowing up and throwing acid on a zombie sounds pretty damn cool but not that practical. Flamethrowers seem great, but how many people have access to one and even then would know how to use the bloody thing? When you combine that with the fact that zombies don't feel pain and you would then have to deal with flaming zombies, you would be in deep trouble. Zombies, just like people, take a long time to burn, and with them not being able to feel any pain you would most likely just burn yourself.

If you're an explosives expert that has access to explosives, then they might make a great way to secure your perimeter. To the rest of us, they'll probably end up blowing us into a million little pieces, if we can get them to work at all.

Unless you're running around with buckets of acid, I don't think it would be much use at all to anyone. Given enough acid and time I'm sure that you could dig a pit, fill it with acid, then sit around and watch zombies fall in it. Not really practical at all but as a last resort; actually, even then zombies don't feel pain, so how long have you got before the acid does enough damage to kill it? Not long enough.

## *Fight or Flight*

If you had to choose either, flight is always the best option. Avoid contact with zombies or other people as much as possible and live to fight another day. If you have to fight, then fight as if your life depends on it - because it does.

## Chapter Five

# DO IT SOLO OR IN A GROUP

It could be zombies, disease or disaster, but regardless of what it is, you have some important decisions to make. One of those decisions you'll have to make sooner or later is whether to go it alone, lone-wolf style, or team up with a group and pool your resources. There are as many arguments for both sides of this common debate, and I'm not going to say who is wrong or right. What I will try and do is give you a good look at both sides of the story and let you form your opinion from there.

Hollywood has made the idea of going it alone as some sort of hero a very attractive and romantic idea, but in reality it's extremely hard. In much the same way, the group is often made out to be the aggressor in several zombie situations.

## *Lone Wolf Solo Style*

*Advantages*
Getting around quickly alone. Often people think that they will be able to move quicker alone than with a group. If you're on foot in relatively

easy and open terrain, then this might well be accurate. In an urban city location or heavier terrain overcoming obstacles could prove difficult alone but may be much easier if you have help from other people.

You don't need to carry as many supplies if you're alone. That is technically correct to a point, but when you think about it, if everyone carries their own supplies it doesn't matter. If you found yourself in an area with little natural resources, you would use them up slower than a large group. Another thing to consider is that if you're in a base or safe house you may have only enough resources to support one person. If you're searching alone for food and supplies and find nothing, you could go hungry or cold.

If you have a group searching split up, there is more chance of finding what you need to survive.

You create less of a footprint alone. This one is hard to argue against. If you're moving alone you leave fewer signs, make less noise, and leave less waste to be found. You will be able to cover up your camp easier and yourself if you're being hunted.

No one to argue with. Yep, no one disagreeing with you about what to do or which way to go if you're alone. If you're alone, however, you might miss something that another person could see. Also, you are responsible for making decisions when you are cold, tired and hungry, and often this will affect the decision you make.

*Disadvantages*
Loneliness and eventual madness could be a killer just as surely as if a zombie bites you. Some studies have shown that people who go it alone have only a 20% chance of survival compared to 80% when in a group situation. For the most part, people are creatures that need social interaction to remain sane. If you add in the stresses of zombies or other potential hazards that people wouldn't normally encounter when alone, it could potentially be fatal.

You don't have other people to share the watch with or take responsibility for the safety of your perimeter. If you're alone eventually you will need to sleep and even though you may have defenses, you will be at a disadvantage with no one to share the burden with. It's not just sleeping either; toilet breaks, hunting, building, moving – you'll always have to spend longer doing simple tasks because you're alone.

If you become sick or injured, you have no one to help you. You have no one to take up your responsibilities. This leaves you extremely vulnerable to attacks. You will be tired or incapable of moving to resupply or defend yourself.

## Group Situation

*Advantages*

A better overall support system for all activities. You can carry more equipment around, spreading the load among more people. You might not be able to carry everything alone and will have to sacrifice essential equipment. In a group, you have a lot more of a choice in what you carry.

You have a wide range of ideas and suggestions of action when you have many different points of view. Often when you're faced with a difficult decision, having another point of view could be invaluable and save your life. When you're in a stressful situation, your brain doesn't normally function as it would.

A group can share the duties among many people to lighten the load and make the camp or base overall safer. Take your perimeter security for example. One person alone is responsible 24 hours a day. Two people handle 12 hours each day. Six people are only responsible for watch duties 4 hours per day. If you have to gather food or hunt you have better chances with a group divided up into separate parties. This also means people could remain in camp to provide security while other people are hunting.

You have a bigger range of skills with more people around you. You could have special forces, cooks, survivalists, preppers, security personnel, doctors, nurses, farmers, mechanics - the choices are essentially limitless.

When you have a lot of people, it makes it possible to carry a lot more gear and equipment. This means that things that are too heavy or bulky to carry alone, but still extremely useful, can be broken down and spread among the entire group.

*Disadvantages*

If you are in a group, you will always be looking for more supplies. This includes things like food, medical, hygiene ammunition, etc. When you're alone you won't need as much and when you do find a cache of supplies it will last longer.

More people means more opinions and different ways of doing things. If you're alone, then you only have to deal with yourself. When you're in a group, you have to have some form of leadership or democracy that in itself can cause problems.

Noise and an overall bigger footprint make security and concealment a lot harder when you have more people in one area. Eventually, another group may come along and assume you have something worth stealing. This can lead to you increasing the size of your group and them increasing theirs. The more people around, the more food there is for zombies. A lot of people equals a lot of potential zombie food.

You don't have to do it alone or with a group of people you don't know. Your family is a great place to start a group. You could include extended family or friends.

Another idea is to include a dog in your group. This can be a great company if you're alone. Remember that including a dog has a whole new set of problems like noise, food and training to consider.

Ultimately it will be up to you to choose which method you choose to take.

## Chapter Six

# HOW TO FORM A SURVIVAL GROUP

If you have decided to form a survival group, then the best chance you have is to start early. Remember the five P's: Preparation Prevents Piss Poor Performance. No matter what you do in life, this saying will cover almost everything. The variety of different skills and information that individuals bring to a group is a vital element in survival. Forming your group, allocating roles based on experience and then practicing your skills as a group is extremely important. It's not much good if you form a group, but then you never practice. Teams all around the world no matter what their function is work by practicing until they know what each team member can do and it becomes instinct. When you have your team and their roles, people know which areas they can focus and improve on and which skills they can learn as secondary skills. This way, if you lose one member of your team, you have someone ready to step up and fill the void.

For this book we are focusing on a zombie outbreak, but you could always use the same instructions for any number of different scenarios. Now it's time to move onto the essentials to forming a group.

Don't just start by inviting everyone you know to join your group when you first start organizing. There are certain things you need to think about before inviting members into your group. You need to consider how many family members they have, what their goals are and even where they live. Once you know this information you can begin to form your group, and remember that it's easier to invite someone than un-invite them.

First, establish what the aims of your group will be. It doesn't matter if you have twenty people in your group or two, there will always be disagreement. It's how the people in your group deal with arguments and disagreements that really matters. Having different points of view and different opinions is healthy and an advantage to your group. Knowing when it's time to move on without hurt feelings becoming involved in a mature way is the important thing. If everyone understands the aims, goals and rules of the group and can abide by them, there shouldn't be any misunderstandings.

Next you need to know where your team is going. It's easy to suggest a central location to everyone, but this might not be the best idea. You need to think about the needs of your group. The location preferably needs to be isolated, easily securable and big enough to support your group. If you don't have a place like that but know someone who does, then consider them the first person you should approach to join your team. The ideal candidate should be willing to either begin preparing their property now or be willing to let you help them. Establishing crops and animals now is perfect; this way you'll be ready if or when the worst occurs.

Knowing the numbers of your team is one thing, but how many people will they bring with them? Unless every member of your team is single with no family, then most of them will likely want to bring people with them. You need to know how many people each member would like to bring with them while you're forming the group, so you don't invite too many people. Ultimately it will be up to you how many people you allow the members of your group to bring with them. Be aware of the extra resources you will need to allow per person. These are things like sleeping arrangements, food, water and hygiene needs. You will need definite numbers, and every member of the group will need to be made aware that there won't be exceptions made.

Everyone in the group will need to be assigned certain jobs to do within the group. Some of these will ultimately be based upon their particular skills, but even children and group members without skills will need jobs to complete. This is easy to organize as long as people understand their roles and why they're necessary. Outline the tasks that need to be completed make a job board and rotate people through all the tasks.

It doesn't matter how many people you have in your survival group, you'll ultimately need someone to the leader. Someone needs to take responsibility, even though people will often at times resent the leader; it comes with the territory. You could also form a committee, which I'll talk about that next.

A committee is an important way to give every member of the group voice, no matter their role within it. If your committee or whatever you decide to call it functions well, there is almost no need for a leadership position.

Let's talk about some of the different roles you need to consider when you're thinking of inviting people to join your group.

## *Core Group Skills*

- **Security** – The primary roles of team members assigned to security is the overall safety of your group's position. The security force can't just stand around making sure your perimeter is safe; they need to take a more proactive role. They should know who is within a certain distance of your safe location, where the nearest escape routes are and secure water and food resources. Any military, police, emergency services or security personnel are the best choice. If you have more than one or two security people, then you should consider one to be that section leader to report back to the committee.

- **Food & Supplies** – There are a lot of different areas that this category can be broken down into, all of them important. How many people you have in the food section will ultimately depend on how many people you need to provide for in your group. I'll do a quick breakdown of some of the different roles for you:

- **Gardener** – If you have already planted crops then you're off to a good start. If the ground isn't contaminated and the security force can protect your gardeners from zombies or other people looking to take what you have, this is preferred. You need to think of the different varieties of plants such as herbs, fruit and vegetables that you will need. Stockpiling seeds and cultivating different varieties is in your best interests. Do your research and get the hardiest varieties suited to your location. Don't forget to consider what any animals you may have need to eat too.

- **Forager** – Every group needs someone that is skilled in the local plants and trees, knowing which varieties grow wild, where, and what is edible or poisonous.

- **Hunters** – You may not always be able to rely on the domesticated animals that you have. Stocks run low and having a skilled hunter to supplement stores will always be a big advantage to your group.

- **Trappers** – The hunters and trappers will normally work well together. These group members often know the different animals that frequent your area, where they are and how to trap them.

- **Trackers** – Another group member that will work well with the hunters and trappers. They won't just be skilled at tracking animals either. A good tracker will be able to establish who and what is in your area and be able to track humans just as well as any animals.

- **Fisherman** – Often we consider fishing as just a way to relax, but in an emergency situation this could mean the difference between life and death for your group. If you have a source of water nearby that is stocked with fish, your group will never go hungry.

- **Cook / Chef** – Your group will need a cook or chef to prepare meals and help to manage the stores of food. Depending on the size of your group you may either need more than one or the position may be able to be rotated among a few different group members.

- **Doctor / Medic / Nurse** – Often not considered until a group member is dying or sick with no one knowing what to do. A simple cut or infection can be deadly without the correct treatment. If the people in your group don't have medical training, consider asking someone to take first aid courses.

These are probably some of the core skills your group requires if you plan on lasting as long as possible. I'll go into some other often overlooked skills that you may need to consider. All of these people may not make or break your group, but you probably have some of these skills among your group members already.

## *Additional Group Skills*

- **Survival Experts** – Most of your group will already have basic survival skills and interests, but there will always be someone that is more passionate and skilled at it than others. Consider organizing this person to teach other less inclined members of your group survival skills.

- **Mechanics** – Most mechanics will have a general knowledge of engines, not just fixing cars. This could include motorbikes, buggies, generators and other farm machinery.

- **Tradesmen (Plumber, Electrician, Welder, Builder)** – There isn't going to be a phone directory if zombies are rampaging across the world. When things need repairing having any of these tradesmen among your group will prove invaluable.

- **Vets** – Depending on whether you have animals or plan on having them, they will need almost as much care as the group members.

- **Teachers** – If you plan on surviving a long time, you need to consider the needs of any children or future children.

- **Weapons Specialists** – Weapons are great, but if they don't work they aren't much good. Having a group member that is trained in multiple weapons and their maintenance will come in handy.

Now that you have all of your group's positions defined, you can start searching for different people to fill them. Consider having people train in other people's areas as much as possible. This way, if the worst happens you have someone ready to step up and help as best they can.

You need to schedule regular meetings and training sessions to keep your group together. If you're preparing a safe bug-out location, that is a perfect place to hold regular camping/survival weekend and working days. People will become familiar with their surroundings and also feel more of a connection with the location.

Don't just stick to one particular area either; spread out and camp in different areas. Hold training sessions at different times of the year to gain experience no matter what season it is.

During the different weekend trips start slowly. Don't try and push people too hard - once or twice a year, and then build up to more frequent sessions. Run different scenarios, zombies, flood, foreign military, etc. Pick a theme and then have fun with it. Practice different skills, first aid, tracking, hunting, etc. The more your group bonds, the better equipped it will be to handle whatever situation it's faced with.

Good luck and remember to keep it fun, but never forget how serious it could be one day.

## Chapter Seven

# BEST VEHICLES FOR POST-APOCALYPTIC TRAVEL

There are many different things that you need to take into consideration when you're thinking of moving around in a hostile environment full of zombies and other predators. I have already talked about walking or traveling in a vehicle so I'm not going to go into the pros and cons of that specifically again.

What we need to consider firstly is your level of preparation. If and when the dead rise and walk the lands again, have you already prepared your vehicle or are you looking for a vehicle after the event?

If you're just getting out of town with your own personal vehicle or taking whatever is closest, you don't have a lot of choices to begin with. Later on you will be able to either upgrade or swap vehicles depending on what may be available.

If you have the time and money, then you most likely have vehicles prepared. These might be specific vehicles that you have personally specially customized and adapted for post-apocalyptic travel, or you purchased. There is a wide variety of quad bikes, motorbikes, SUV's, trucks, mobile homes and buses that are available for survivalists. What you choose often depends on how much you can afford to spend and how much room you have to store the vehicle.

I'm not going to review all of the different models. What I will try and do is cover some of the pros and cons of different types of vehicles.

So let's break this down into a general list of different types of transportation.

- Cars
- Trucks / SUV
- Buses / Campers / Mobile Homes
- Motorcycles & Quadbikes
- Bicycles

All motorized vehicles make noise that can more often than not attract unwanted attention from both zombies and people looking to take what you have.

## *Cars*

Cars provide you with extra capabilities to carry more equipment and supplies but only offer limited areas in which you can operate. Most cars have low ground clearance so you will be forced to use roads, highways and tracks that can often leave you vulnerable. They aren't as noisy as motorcycles or trucks that may give you a slight edge. Have you ever slept in a car? There not the most relaxing place to sleep either, but could be better than spending a night out in the open.

## *Trucks or SUV*

More space to carry equipment or people is always a bonus. They also require more fuel to operate which could become a burden. Scavenging for fuel means going into places where people are or used to be, and that means more zombies. More room gives you a bit of extra room to escape the biters and bad weather. Trucks and SUVs can go places that cars can't, which gives you a lot more options when it comes to where you go.

## Buses / Campers / Mobile Homes

More people means added strength and security, but it also means you need to resupply more often which means risky scavenging. Having a mobile place to live and defend means that you won't get stuck in one place if you run out of recourses but also requires more fuel to operate. Being bigger and stronger than cars or trucks means that you could turn these vehicles into very fortified bases of operation. They're also a lot harder to hide than smaller vehicles if you need to keep a low profile. You may outrun zombies or people on foot, but you're limited to bigger well-surfaced roads, and you won't out run bikes, cars or trucks.

## Motorcycles & Quadbikes

The sky is the limit to where you can go on either of these vehicles. They are quick and small, meaning you'll be able to hide them a lot easier than other vehicles. Not as heavy on fuel use like the rest, but most models can be considerably noisier. You are limited to one or two people at the most, and you'll also be limited with the amount of gear you can carry. There isn't a lot of protection from zombies, people or the elements, so you'll be forced to camp outside or in other defensive buildings.

## Bicycles

They might not seem as cool as the other vehicles, but a good bike will definitely beat walking all over the countryside. You will be limited to just yourself and the equipment you can carry, but silence is definitely an advantage in keeping a low profile. They don't offer much in the way of protection from people, zombies or the elements, so you'll be forced to find somewhere safe of a night or day to sleep. Another advantage to a bicycle is that it can be easily disassembled and carried over rougher terrain. Easy to repair, no fuel costs and most parts that need to be replaced can be carried with you easily.

# Chapter Eight

## ZOMBIE MISCONCEPTIONS

Without a hundred-percent surety, there will always be different versions and ideas surrounding zombies. From what they look like to how they act, there is a hell of a lot of different zombies running or stumbling around out there. Don't be fooled by common mistakes that could just get you killed, or worse infected.

One of the best things you could do is perhaps save one bullet for yourself if things get desperate. No one wants to turn into a zombie, destined to walk the earth searching for something, slowly rotting away.

Hopefully, some of the following common myths and misconceptions will give you the edge you need in your own battle against the undead.

### *Misconception One*

According to the many different versions of Vodoun or Haitian Voodoo a person who has been brought back from the dead by a Bokor can be controlled. They believe that by feeding this zombie salt, it will send them back to their grave. This has never been confirmed and doesn't exactly sound like my idea of a fun night.

## *Misconception Two*

Zombies are only interested in eating your brains. This trend of brain-eating zombies started in the movie The Return of the Living Dead and still keeps coming around. If this was the case, then I know a couple of people that could walk around all day without any worries at all. Unfortunately for us, most zombies won't just stop with brains - they want it all.

## *Misconception Three*

It has been suggested that zombies will rise and walk the earth when Hell has reached its maximum capacity. I'm not sure if Hotel Hell exists or not and if it has a maximum capacity, but I don't think it's kicking out its guests just yet.

## *Misconception Four*

Some people believe that our walking dead friends can speak, but this is highly unlikely. Most viral or bacterial infections that could cause a person to turn into a zombie, specifically target the brain or brain stem. This allows very limited functions to existing, walking, biting, sight and hearing for the most part. Most zombies are for the most part uncoordinated at best and unlikely to speak or use any sort of tools. They are more likely to use their own heads to smash their way through any sort of barrier.

## *Misconception Five*

Many people believe that zombies are some sort of monster. This isn't true though they may exhibit monstrous behavior. A true monster is something created; zombies after all were once humans. Besides, monsters aren't real, and we all know that zombies are extremely real.

## *Misconception Six*

Some folks like to consider that zombies are immortal creatures. They might not die like us because mostly they're already dead, but they can most certainly be killed. Take out the brain or brain stem and you'll see how immortal they aren't.

## *Misconception Seven*

Zombies are not capable of being cured. In most cases from everything we know zombies can't be cured and almost everyone that is bitten or scratched turns. There will obviously always be a small percentage of the population with immunity, but I wouldn't bet my life on it if I had a choice. In some cases, a rapid amputation of the affected area if possible may stop the infection from spreading. This is shown in World War Z and the Living Dead.

## *Misconception Eight*

Zombies would make great pets, not! Why would you take the risks trying to domesticate a zombie? The number of cons here definitely outweighs any advantages. In the Walking Dead the character played by Danai Gurira, Michonne, is commonly seen with two zombies she leads around as pets. They have their fingers and teeth removed so that they can't bite, and this leads them to be almost docile. She uses these "tame" zombies to move around other zombies. I wouldn't recommend it myself!

## *Misconception Nine*

Zombies aren't the dead risen from the graves. The zombie virus needs a living victim for it to survive. Otherwise, the first few zombies would just eat themselves, and that would be the end of it.

There are hundreds of different zombie movies and television shows available for you to watch. Some are funny, some are serious and some are just plain stupid. I'm not going to write an in-depth review of all of them. Instead, I will just try and break some of them down a little bit for you, plot, type of zombies and their characteristics.

## *World War Z 2013*

An epidemic sweeps across the world with the origin unknown initially. The main character, after escaping the initial outbreak, tries to track down where the virus initiated from and attempts to find a cure. No cure is discovered, but he discovers that the zombies aren't interested in victims that have terminal illnesses. Using this discovery, they create a type of camouflage, infecting themselves with a deadly disease to help them remain hidden from the zombies, enabling them to fight back.

- Zombie Characteristics – Fast and agile
- Zombie Cause – Believed initially to be a rabies variation from China. 12 seconds from being bitten to becoming a zombie
- Cures / Immunization – Infection with a deadly disease can shield you from the zombies
- Location – Worldwide

## *The Walking Dead 2010 – Current*

A sheriff awakens from a coma to discover that the world has been swept away by a zombie pandemic. The story continues with him struggling to survive while he searches for his son and wife and his struggles along with those of his group of survivors.

- Zombie Characteristics – Reasonably fast
- Zombie Cause – Unclear
- Cures / Immunization – None at this point. An interesting point here is that the actual zombie virus doesn't make you a zombie. The zombie virus is airborne, and everyone is already contaminated; the zombie bite kills you, then you return as a

zombie. No matter how you die, you will return as a zombie because you're already infected
- Location – Worldwide

## *The Return of the Living Dead 1985*

A classic zombie brain-eating comedy horror combination. Two employees in a medical facility accidentally release a toxic gas that causes the dead to rise and walk the earth.

- Zombie Characteristics – Slow
- Zombie Cause – Toxic gas release
- Cures / Immunization
- Location – Louisville, Kentucky, USA

## *Resident Evil 2002*

Inside a secret laboratory facility known as "The Hive," a virus escapes and infects the medical staff, turning them into zombies. The computer system attempts to lock down the lab to prevent the infection until the company sends in security forces to clean up the mess. Eventually, the virus manages to escape and then infects the rest of the world.

- Zombie Characteristics – Fast variations and slow
- Zombie Cause – Escaped T-Virus
- Cures / Immunization – There could be up to four cures, but they are only effective at the beginning of infection
- Location – Worldwide

## *28 Days Later 2002*

A mysterious virus spreads across the United Kingdom. Originally started when animal activists release chimpanzees that were contaminated with the "Rage" virus. The main character wakes up from a coma to discover his country ravaged by the virus and has to try to navigate his way across the land.

- Zombie Characteristics – Fast, aggressive
- Zombie Cause – Rage virus from laboratory experiments
- Cures / Immunization – None. Some people are immune to the effects of the rage virus but can still infect others
- Location – United Kingdom

## *I Am Legend 2007*

The main character is a scientist who cannot stop the spread of the virus that is quickly tearing through the world. He stays alone for many years trying to find a cure to the disease using his immune blood and samples taken from zombies.

- Zombie Characteristics – Fast, but sensitive to daylight
- Zombie Cause – Man-made virus
- Cures / Immunization – Potentially
- Location – United States

## Chapter Nine

# ZOMBIE SURVIVAL TIPS TO KEEP YOU ALIVE

In this part, we're going to try and give you a big list of tips that you'll be able to quickly reference and soak in. It's pretty obvious that all round the world things are starting to change rapidly. Mass shootings, disease and virus outbreaks, civil wars and uprisings are all increasing at a rapid pace. It may not have happened yet, but all it takes is a scientist or group to mess around with the wrong genetics or vaccinations and we'll have a zombie apocalypse situation. Here are some great zombie survival tips that will help keep you and your loved ones alive!

### *Be Cautious of Other Survivors*

Once you get used to zombies, you're going to be able to predict their behavior and react accordingly. Believe it or not, zombies may not be your biggest problem. Other survivors are unpredictable and you can never be 100% sure what their intentions will be: good or bad. If you have something they need, or want, they may be unpredictable and dangerous. It's always a good idea to approach other survivors with your head on a swivel.

## *Build Alliances with Other Survivors*

It's important to remember the first point we made when you approach other survivors. You want to increase your group and have other survivors around you, but you don't want to be robbed or killed. You can't watch and sleep at the same time and more people means you'll be able to spread hunting, gathering and security work out further among more survivors.

## *Don't Drop Your Guard*

Just because you think that your new allies are okay, don't be lulled into a false sense of security. It's important that you keep your guard up and make sure that you don't get taken advantage of. There will be differences of opinion and tension whenever different groups get together, regardless of the situation. If you don't believe that you're going to be able to move past the differences, then you may want to think about moving on before you get too entangled.

## *Think About Building a Base of Operations*

Before you start looking around and exploring, you're going to want to ensure that you have a strong base of operations to fall back on. Secure your location and then start looking around. It may take a few days, or weeks, but if you have a strong base of operations to fall back on when anything goes wrong, you'll be much safer. There are certain things that you want to think about when you're scouting out different locations for your base. You'll need a secure and well-defendable area first and foremost. Access to escape routes if you need to bug out in a hurry, and preferably somewhere that has easy access to a water source. Just remember, if an area looks good to you, other survivors may find it attractive also, and they aren't always friendly!

## The Division of Work Among Survivors

It's always important that everyone in a survival group contributes to work and chores, or has skills which they can contribute to the group. If everyone works together to help out, then the group will have more time and energy to focus on improvements and the security of the alliance. It's important that you establish which people are suited to which tasks, and that you divide the different tasks equally so that one person or another doesn't feel overworked.

## Remember, You're Still Alive

It's important that you remember that you're still alive and that life is still continuing. Survival will be tough and there won't be a lot of spare time, but there may be opportunities to relax, even if it's only for a few minutes. While television and radio may be out, there are always good old paperback books to fall back on. Instruction manuals and textbooks may seem boring, but learning any new skill could come in handy one day.

## Learn New Things

If you have people in the group that are skilled hunters, then it's important for them to teach other people the skill of hunting. If anything was to happen to that one person, then the group would be left without a skilled hunter. Every role in the group should have someone that could serve as a backup in the case of an emergency or accident.
ruits and vegetables would be an extremely valuable skill to have in any survival situation.

## Keep the Zombie Population Down

While you don't always want to go out and kill zombies, or actively pursue dangerous zombie fighting situations, it is a necessary evil. You want to ensure, first and foremost, that zombies around your immediate base are kept well clear. This could mean building lanes or barriers that will steer zombies away, or keeping a zombie-free zone around the base camp. While it sucks that you're killing zombies that were once people, unless there is a cure in the immediate future, it's better to be safer rather than sorry. It's always better to fight one or two zombies more often, than large groups of ten, twenty, or one hundred zombies.

## *Know Your Area of Operations*

It's important that you have a good knowledge of your local area and the situation in the area that you're working in. You need to know when something isn't right or who else may be in the area. Knowledge is priceless! If you don't have maps, then either scavenge some or develop your own maps. Record accesses into your areas and also plan out escape routes. If you have buildings or locations where you have found useful food or equipment, then record them so that you can return at later dates or send out other members of the group.

## *Repairing Infrastructure*

Unfortunately, one of the first things that collapses in any emergency situation is infrastructure. Power, fuel, energy and communications all rapidly breakdown. While you may not be able to establish or repair power stations and communications, you can work on creating your own energy sources. Salvaging solar panels and wind-generating devices is a great way to create efficient, renewable and, most importantly, quiet sources of energy. Generators should only be used in an emergency situation or for limited amounts of time. They require fuel, which will be hard to source and maintain, as well as creating a lot of noise. A lot of noise may not attract the visitors that you want!

## Chapter Ten

# ZOMBIES THAT YOU'RE LIKELY TO ENCOUNTER

We have already spoken about the four main types of zombies. Now we're going to talk about the different zombies that you're likely to encounter in any post-apocalyptic zombie wasteland. We collected this list of zombies from popular books, television shows and movies. There are sure to be some we missed, but we tried to focus on the most common types of zombies that you would be likely to encounter during any zombie apocalypse scenario.

The majority of zombies aren't going to break any intelligence records, but they make up for this lack of brain function with numbers. Outsmarting them isn't going to be your biggest problem. Getting trapped or swarmed by large numbers is always the major concern. If you can avoid it, always try to keep an escape path open. You don't want to be backing yourselves into a corner and having no way to get out.

## The **Generic Zombie** we all know and love (or loathe)

This is your standard zombie. Someone that has contracted the disease or been bitten by a zombie and reanimated that way. They are normally pretty stupid, but make up for their lack of smarts by safety in numbers. Aggressive, and about average speed. When you are squaring off with one or two you should be fine, but always be aware of what's around you!

## The **Walkers** or **Walking Zombies**

You'll most likely encounter Walkers in shows such as *The Walking Dead*, *Killing Floor*, and the *Night of The Living Dead*. They aren't going to win any 100m sprints, but a horde of Walkers will start to give you some serious health problems. Staying power is right up there, so put them down hard and fast and keep your wits about you.

## The sneaky fast ones or **Runners**

These zombies are going to cause you some serious headaches! Runners are going to chase you down and it's going to take some serious firepower to bring them down. Some people believe that runners are fresh zombies, with many of their human capabilities intact. Don't try and outrun them, you'll just die tired. Runners quickly move from person to person, bringing them down and then moving onto new victims. If you can't kill them outright, try and take out their legs. You'll see Runners in movies like *28 Days Later*, *REC 2*, *Left 4 Dead*, *World War Z* and *Dawn of the Dead* (2004).

## The classic **Romero Zombies**

Romero Zombies are zombies that are found in the films by George A. Romero. Many consider Romero as a pioneer for what we all consider zombies to be today. The most important part of Romero's Zombies is that they have the ability to learn and adapt. There is nothing scarier than a zombie, right? Wrong! A zombie which can learn and adapt is the scariest thing walking the planet!

## *The walking **Infected/Contaminated** Zombies*

Either way, zombies are bad news. Infected or Contaminated zombies are an altogether new level of high-risk. When it comes to Infected or Contaminated Zombies, you'll want to take extreme care with fluids or blood and brain splatter. You want to ensure that you're covering your face, hands and any other exposed wounds. If you can, engage them at a distance and use extreme care when disposing of any bodies. A biological or chemical suit is going to come in handy, but remember that it's going to slow you down and hinder movement and reflexes.

## *The **Crawlers***

They might not seem as dangerous as Walkers or Runners, but these annoying zombies are sure to pack one hell of a bite if you're not paying attention. They won't walk up on you, but they will crawl up and grab you if you're not ready. Disabled from the torso down, these mutilated zombies are forced to drag themselves around looking for helpless victims or scarps. You'll find crawlers in almost every zombie film, book or television show. The worst thing about crawlers is that, nine times out of ten, you'll walk into one of them, not the other way around.

## *Those **Spitters, Vomiters** and **Pukers***

You'll want to give these zombies a wide berth. When it comes to all three, there's going to be some serious bodily fluid flying around. You still have to be aware of teeth, but their primary way of infection is going to be bodily fluids. Keep these guys and girls at arm's reach; long-handled weapons are preferred. If you see zombies with excessive amounts of drool, or vomit around their mouths, it's an indication that some toxic zombie fluids could be coming your way. If you're in an area with an abundant amount of any three of these zombies, an industrial facemask of some type would be a wise investment.

## *Those clever* **Stalkers**

The Stalkers won't just eat you, they're going to track you down and enjoy doing it! The zombies are normally crawling around on all fours, keeping them closer to the ground as this is better for following scent. It's also going to make seeing them more difficult. They aren't as fast as other zombies but, because of their low profile they will be harder to kill. Don't allow them to get too close; they could spring or leap at you.

## *Evil* **Nazi Zombies**

Just like the name suggests, these Zombies are the dead Nazi soldiers come back to walk the lands and cause chaos again! They're easy to identify, with their Nazi uniforms hanging tattered on their rotting remains.

## Conclusion

Thanks for taking the time to read my book, I hope that you enjoy reading it as much as I enjoyed writing it. Please feel free to contact me with any suggestions or comments, as I love to hear from my readers. My email address is benandsamauthors@gmail.com

If you have a couple of minutes to spare then please take the opportunity to review my book.

Thanks once again,

Ben Jackson.
P.S. Keep safe, and don't get bitten!!!

If you're interested in becoming a prepper or just curious about what you should have in any disaster situation, then you need to make sure you read this!

# References

http://www.popularmechanics.com/science/health/g1216/10-awesome-accidental-discoveries/

http://zombease.com/survival-guides/anti-zombie-weapons-and-defense/

http://www.livescience.com/40690-zombie-haiti-are-zombies-real.html

http://content.time.com/time/specials/packages/article/0,28804,2008962_2008964_2008992,00.html

http://www.livescience.com/48386-deadliest-viruses-on-earth.html

http://www.planetdeadly.com/human/deadliest-poisons-man

http://survivalcache.com/bug-out-bag/

http://www.thebugoutbagguide.com/2014/09/17/how-to-pack-your-bug-out-bag/

http://www.practicalsurvivor.com/waterfiltration

http://survivalathome.com/homemade-mres/

http://survivalcache.com/survival-debate-group-survival-solo-survival/

http://www.wikihow.com/Create-a-Survival-Group

http://survivalathome.com/how-to-build-your-own-survival-team/

http://zombie.wikia.com/wiki/Transportation

http://401ak47.com/10-myths-about-zombies/

http://www.imdb.com/?ref_=nv_home

http://www.who.int/mediacentre/factsheets/fs360/en/

http://zombie.wikia.com/wiki/Types_of_Zombies

http://www.lolwot.com/20-useful-tips-for-surviving-a-zombie-apocalypse/5/

Printed in Great Britain
by Amazon